Redefining Marriage

MARRIED TO THE ~~EGO~~ SOUL

Tori Player

Redefining Marriage

Copyright © 2019 Tori Player
All rights reserved. No part of this publication may be reproduced, distributed, or transmitted in any form or by any means, including photocopying, recording, or other electronic or mechanical methods, without the prior written permission of the publisher, except in the case of brief quotations embodied in critical reviews and certain other noncommercial uses permitted by copyright law.

ISBN-13: 978-1-970079-22-7
ISBN 1-970079-22-3

Published by Opportune Independent Publishing Company

Opportune Publishing is a full-service book publishing company that focuses on non-traditional authorship. It is our business to keep a diligent emphasis on quality and precision, while always allowing innovation and creativity to seep through. Unlike many other publishing companies, all genres are welcomed here.

For permission requests, write to the publisher, addressed "Atention: Permissions Coordinator" to the address below.

Email: Info@opportunepublishing.com
Address: 113 N. Live Oak Street
Houston, TX 77003

Redefining Marriage

Foreword

I have learned a great deal about myself in the past few years primarily because I was faced with a challenge that made me explore things I never considered.

I had been married for ten years and raising two beautiful children, yet there was no joy, passion or fulfillment in my heart. To say it succinctly, I was empty, depleted and discouraged and yearning for more.

By opening my heart and mind, I was inspired by that still small voice that speaks to us all from within. It started slowly, prompting me in a new direction and fortunately, I was paying attention. That message held up a mirror to me and revealed what I was doing to myself and how I could stop the self-sabotage.

I was guided down a spiritual and emotional healing journey that helped me unearth the truth about myself, about love and about marriage. I found myself and became a stronger person within and without through the healing power of love.

Fueled with purpose, passion and peace, my life took a meaningful turn going from darkness to light and helping me evolve into a higher version

Redefining Marriage

of myself. It was through these truths that I learned what marriage really means and what it is meant to be for the two individuals that enter into this sacred partnership.

I hope you will read these pages with an open heart and an open mind and allow it to give you the intended gift you deserve….the gift of genuine love.

Introduction

Times have dramatically changed, yet unfortunately our approach to marriage has largely stayed the same. Sure, we'd like to think we're marrying for love but why then is the divorce rate so high? Why is infidelity still running rampant? I believe it is because we marry from an unconscious and superficial place. In other words, we marry each other's ego. The ego has us focused on many self-serving reasons such as lustful relationships, expectations, finances, security and societal concepts.

However, we've reached a point in time where our reasons for marrying should be evaluated more carefully. As a starting off place, women should be viewed as far more than just those who **raise children, cook, clean, and provide sex**. And we've certainly reached a point where men need to be viewed as much more than **providers**.

Our view of marriage needs a major overhaul for marriage requires a new direction and focus. By a new direction and focus, I mean we need to **create a skill set that helps us move past the ego so as to build unions that are soul focused, abundant, intentional, and fortified with deep intimacy.**

Redefining Marriage

If you are jumping the broom soon, or dreaming about jumping the broom, this book is for you. It is designed to expand your mind and inspire you to cultivate a conscious and sustainable self-loving, healthy, and harmonious relationship that you and your partner can share and enjoy. I recommend working through this book with your partner so that it sparks conversation and ignites a love that lies deep within.

I hope you find true value in this book, for as you use the specific principles outlined, they can help you build a **successful marriage.** These particular principles were never taught to me…not even in premarital counseling. Rather, it was through my own personal experience that I gained the necessary insight to bring this important message to you. So, let's begin!

Chapter 1
Shedding the Ego

`Oh, how the ego deceives us!` It will have us thinking we are something we're not, telling us lies and blocking the very truth of who we really are. It creates illusions and sadly, a false sense of love. The ego controls and lives in the mind, building a wall around the heart. If we don't actively work to dissolve it, it will create unwanted circumstances and situations that cause nothing but chaos and distraction.

Where Does The Ego Come From?

To understand the hold of the ego, we have to understand the ego. We enter into this world as an extremely bright, shining light. We have an energy about us that gives off good vibes of **pure light, love, and joy.** However, as soon as we are born, we enter into a world where the mind is dominated by ego. Ego is the idea or opinion we have of ourselves or our importance as a person. Society lives and operates in ego whether it's from our parents' parents passing down their ego, to what we learn from the media, and so on and so on and so on.

We are taught through ego, and soon we

become our very own version of ego. We bring ego into our schools, relationships and work life, and for those that have children, we pass it on to them. And so it becomes this vicious cycle of living in **insecurity, fear, negative emotions, lack and limitation.** This is all unhealthy energy that we bring into our marriages.

Conversely, when we know who we are at a soul level, when we learn how to decipher the difference between soul and ego, we are then in a position to create **greater lives, greater experiences, greater love, and greater marriages.** Knowing yourself, **loving yourself**, and understanding yourself is the beginning of all things good.

Developing The Soul

We start by understanding the soul. **The soul is the true essence of you.** Your soul is your true home. It is pure, positive, loving energy. It houses your dreams, your desires, your visions, your passions, and what you believe and value. **A healthy and nourished soul will always lead to a happy and nourished life.** When the focus is on developing and growing the soul, it automatically deprives the ego. A wonderful mantra to live by is, **"Feed the soul; starve the ego."**

Chapter 2
The Spirit of Marriage

Marriage is **spiritual and sacred**. It is a responsibility and commitment that says **we honor each other's heart, we nourish each other's soul and we respect each other's minds.** If we are to commit to "death do us part," then a marriage has to offer something that goes beyond the surface, beyond the physical realm and beyond the ego, so that it touches the deepest part of ourselves.

Know Thy Self/Know Thy Mate

To know thyself is the **greatest gift you can give yourself.** Why is it so important to know who you are? If you're entering into a relationship with your ego as the dominant force, how can you create something deep, lasting, and authentic when the ego is deceptive? Two egos marrying each other can be compared to **playing in the kiddie pool for all of your lives.**

The ego will try and hold you there because it has created a false sense of safety and security within the marriage. The thing about ego is that it's **always looking for a place to hide your dark side** and to make you feel safe; so it searches for someone who won't challenge your insecurities, your fears, doubts, and worries.

Over time the ego will just sit there boiling and festering, doing its work until it eventually sabotages the relationship one way or another. Aside from that fact, a lack of knowledge about who you are can lead to a loss of identity. You end up identifying with the roles of marriage more than identifying with the core of who you are.

To alleviate the loss of identity, it's important to know what **emotional baggage** you're bringing to the marriage.

Understanding what you're bringing to the table will prevent you from making your problems your mate's problems or putting pressure on your mate to solve your problems for you. Your mate is there to support, give sound advice, and guide you but your mate will never be able to do the work for you. It is critically important that you are mindful of that premise.

Learning about yourself is an ongoing process. As long as you're breathing you have been blessed with an opportunity to know a little more about who you are each day. Creating a deep intimate relationship with yourself will help you **develop a deep intimate bond with your partner.** And a relationship that speaks to each other's soul is pure bliss!

Keep in mind that you are two individuals with

different paths who are journeying through life together. As your stories unfold on this incredible journey together, your souls will continue to grow towards each other, eventually uniting as one and **creating true harmony and alignment.**

Redefining Marriage

Chapter 3
An Exercise for You and Your Partner

This is a fun and loving exercise that will help you build more conscious awareness towards you and your partner. The following set of questions will guide you beyond the surface, drawing attention to your deeper self.

Instructions

1. Fill out one set of questions for yourself
2. Fill out one set of questions to see how deeply you know your mate
3. Let your partner fill out questions to see how deeply he/she knows you!

Have fun exploring, learning, and growing!

Redefining Marriage

Questions to Answer about Yourself

If you could be doing anything in the world right now, what would you be doing?

What's stopping you from doing this?

What makes you uncomfortable?

Redefining Marriage

Are you aware of any insecurities or fears? If so, list them below.

What do you dream about?

What would you like to experience in this lifetime? These are the desires of your heart. Please list them below.

How do you take care of yourself?

Mentally:

Spiritually:

Physically:

Redefining Marriage

What drains your energy?

How do you pour into yourself so you can pour into your partner and others?

Do you have healthy boundaries established for yourself? If so, what are they?

What are the things you like to do outside of your partnership?

What ultimate vision do you have for yourself at this point in life?

How Well Do You Know Your Partner?

If your partner could be doing anything in the world right now, what would he/she be doing?

Redefining Marriage

What's stopping your partner from doing this?

What makes your partner uncomfortable?

Are you aware of any insecurities or fears? List them below.

What does your partner dream about?

What would your partner like to experience in this lifetime? These are the desires of your heart. Please list them below.

How does your partner take care of his/herself?

Mentally:

Redefining Marriage

Spiritually:

Physically:

What drains your partner's energy?

How does your partner pour into his/herself so he/she can pour into you and others?

Does your partner have healthy boundaries established for his/herself? If so, what are they?

What are the things your partner likes to do outside of the partnership?

What ultimate vision does your partner have for his/herself at this point in life?

How Well Do You Know Yourself?
(For Your Partner to Answer)

If you could be doing anything in the world right now, what would you be doing?

What's stopping you from doing this?

What makes you uncomfortable?

Are you aware of any insecurities or fears? List them below.

What do you dream about?

Redefining Marriage

What would you like to experience in this lifetime? These are the desires of your heart. Please list below.

How do you take care of yourself?

Mentally:

Spiritually:

Physically:

What drains your energy?

How do you pour into yourself so you can pour into your partner and others?

Redefining Marriage

Do you have healthy boundaries established for yourself? If so, what are they?

What are the things you like to do outside of your partnership?

What ultimate vision do you have for yourself at this point in life?

How Well Does Your Partner Know You?
(Questions for your partner to answer about you)

If your partner could be doing anything in the world right now, what would he/she be doing?

What's stopping your partner from doing this?

What makes your partner uncomfortable?

Redefining Marriage

Is your partner aware of any insecurities or fears? List them below.

What does your partner dream about?

What would your partner like to experience in this lifetime? These are the desires of your heart. Please list them below.

How does your partner take care of his/herself?

Mentally:

Spiritually:

Physically:

What drains your partner's energy?

How does your partner pour into his/herself so he/she can pour into you and others?

Does your partner have healthy boundaries established for his/herself? If so, what are they?

What are the things your partner likes to do outside of the partnership?

What ultimate vision does your partner have for his/herself at this point in life?

Redefining Marriage

Beliefs and Values

Beliefs and values are a state of mind in which governs your life. An awareness of each other's beliefs and values encourages a higher level of support and understanding towards each other when it comes to achieving you own personal dreams, goals, and vision. Knowing what's important to each other at a core level is vital to a thriving union.

Exercise for you and your partner:

What's in your Belief and Value System?

Instructions:

1. Circle your top 20 beliefs and values that resonate with you.
2. Have your partner circle their top 20 beliefs and values that resonate with him/her.

Redefining Marriage

For You (Circle your top 20 core beliefs and values)

Logic   Simplicity   Intuition   Perseverance
Power   Education   Humor   Consistency
Faith   Acceptance   Honesty   Freedom
Enthusiasm   Growth   Dreaming   Balance
Wealth   Health   Happiness   Justice
Accountability   Mastery   Generosity
Adventure   Wisdom   Creativity   Daring(risk)
Imagination   Playfulness   Bravery   Peace
Experience   Silence   Optimism   Patience
Community   Determination   Resilience
Open-Mindedness

Are you aligned with and living what you believe and value? Explain.

Redefining Marriage

For your Partner (Circle your top 20 core beliefs and values)

Logic   Simplicity   Intuition   Perseverance
Power   Education   Humor   Consistency
Faith   Acceptance   Honesty   Freedom
Enthusiasm   Growth   Dreaming
Balance   Wealth   Health   Happiness
Determination   Accountability   Mastery
Generosity   Adventure   Wisdom   Creativity
Daring(risk)   Imagination   Playfulness   Bravery
Experience   Silence   Justice   Optimism
Patience   Community   Open-Mindedness
Resilience   Peace

Are you aligned with and living what you believe and value? Explain.

Redefining Marriage

Chapter 4
Building a Strong Foundation
(Friends First, Lovers Second)

Building a foundation of **true friendship** is the key to having a successful union. A solid relationship has to be more than physical for relationships to flourish. **Your emotional and spiritual needs are as important as your physical needs.**

In a true friendship there is no judgment, shame, guilt, jealousy, manipulation, or control, but instead, genuine friendship allows you to **unapologetically express who you are fully and completely.**

When expressing who you are there is a great mix of self-love, unconditional love, trust, high quality communication, engagement, space, giving and receiving, laughter, thoughtfulness, harmony, optimism, and encouragement.

When it comes to creating relationships there are only two types you can create. One is a relationship that drains and the other is a relationship that gives. And while things may not always flow perfectly, as long as you're **consistently striving for a feel good and supportive union,** then the strong foundation you lay will be able to weather any storm.

By way of example, we will now dive into the type of relationship the ego creates and then follow up by exploring the type of relationship that is created when living from the soul.

EGOIC RELATIONSHIP

Judging, Guilt, & Shame

When you judge or criticize your partner for what they think, feel or say, you're sending out a signal that says "I don't honor or respect your difference of opinion." This is how a person coming from an egoic point of view functions and is an automatic rejection of their partner. Placing guilt and shame on your partner for wanting to go outside of the ordinary, or even just wanting to go hang out and have some alone time for example, can cause a lot of suffering in the relationship. What you're actually doing is closing off your partner and making them feel caged.

Blame

Whenever negative emotions and feelings arise and you begin to point the finger at your partner, it is a great opportunity for you to **learn more about yourself.**

Pointing the finger at your partner and blaming

them for making you feel negative emotions is a good time for you to look within yourself and see where that very thing you're blaming your partner for shows up in you. Remember, the ego likes to hide and protect itself so it will always disguise itself and put the negative attention back on someone or something other than you.

Control and Manipulation

Using control and manipulation in a relationship can be silent and sneaky or it can be loud and bold.

The kind I'd like to address now is the silent and sneaky form of control and manipulation for it can be brutal. Quiet control and manipulation is very dangerous because it is more of an unconscious act that can go unnoticed for years before feeling the damage and hurt it has created.

Let's suppose your partner wants to learn how to fly an airplane, since it's always been a dream of theirs. You on the other hand are not that interested in planes and are a bit fearful of your partner learning to fly a plane. So rather than speaking the truth, you approach the subject with a manipulative maneuver and say to your partner, "I don't think we have the money for that right now." You've just limited your partner as they put the thought to rest. This is an ego tactic that focuses on something outside (money) to avoid speaking about how you really feel.

A better and more effective approach might be: "I'm really afraid of you flying planes but I value what makes you happy." If your partner wants to try new things or something outside of the ordinary or vice versa, we must show up with as much love, support, and understanding for each other as possible.

Mother/Father Syndrome

Marriages can quickly turn into a parent/child relationship. An example would be a mother/son relationship or a father/daughter relationship where one is treating the other person like a child. This way of being brings a sense of inferior/superior energy into the mix and makes the other person feel as if they need permission to go here and there. Additionally, having one person make all the important decisions in the relationship creates a huge imbalance, which will result in drowning out the other's voice. You are a team; you are equal, so honor each other's opinions and truly listen to what the other person has to say. **Respect for each other's point of view goes a long way.**

Neediness

You want to be able to **develop a secure place**

within yourself, a place that allows you to emotionally stand on your own. To be truly happy, you must rely on yourself for happiness, for company, and for keeping YOU entertained. Anything outside of yourself is icing on the cake and should add to your life rather than being the reason you exist.

Be careful not to use your partner as a tool to fill any emptiness and voids within you.

Knowing that you are okay and content within yourself makes you a whole person. Rather than feeling the need to unconsciously drain the other person of emotions, feeling okay within yourself allows you to maintain a happy and fulfilled place. If this weren't the case, you would constantly need someone to stroke your ego for the ego needs to feel wanted and loved CONSTANTLY whereas the soul knows it's already loved…period.

Redefining Marriage

Chapter 5
Soulful Relationships

The soul encourages inward growth and it needs space. In other words, it needs room to breathe, and **enjoys exploring the desires that live within the heart.** Carving out alone time to listen to your inner voice is just as important as spending time with and connecting to your partner.

The soul is constantly shifting and guiding you towards growth, so encourage "me" time and create an environment where you make each other feel comfortable about taking time for yourselves. Balance is the key. That way, you're able to come back together stronger, pouring into the marriage with more clarity, insight, and adventure.

Sex, Power, Sacred Energy
Remember this when you get married

- Sex is not entitled to you.
- Sex is not to be rationed out.
- Sex is not a duty.

Always remember quality over quantity. Take time to make love to each other outside of the bedroom, both mentally and spiritually. There is a lot of guilt, shame, and manipulation associated with sex since a lot of us assume that when we get married, sex is entitled to us. We feel that sex is ours anytime we want it and are made to feel like we're obligated to give sex whenever it's asked of us. Magazines and society have encouraged us into believing that we need to meet a certain quota each week in order to keep our mate satisfied and happy. A structured sex life closes off spontaneous energy that actually wards off sexual arousal.

Sex is closely tied to communication. It is an expression of sacred energy and love transferred to each other. We often hear that communication is the key to a good marriage but it is never really addressed or explained in a deeper way.

Let's address it now!

Healthy Communication

Healthy communication involves engaging with each other and providing active listening. The keywords here are: Active and Listening. I like to look at engaged conversation as though you were watching a tennis match. Consider the following:

Is the conversation flowing and going back and forth?

Are you both engaged in the conversation asking questions that go deeper or does the ball get dropped?

Is it a one-sided conversation where you're hardly leaving any room for your mate to participate on a deeper level?

Do you know when it's good to just actively listen to your partner and be fully present with the words your partner is communicating?

Sometimes we look like we're listening to our partner but our minds are actually somewhere else in or out of the room. **Active listening brings a deep level of intimacy** to the relationship, building trust and comfort, and creating a safe place to truly be heard. Ineffective communication and listening will eventually cause a drain on the relationship.

Fully appreciating the other person's expression and thought is truly a gift and a treasure.

We all deserve to be heard, seen and felt, and in marriage it is important to cultivate an environment that reflects that without judgment. **Making each other feel safe always enhances the relationship** and never takes away from it.

Thoughtfulness

Thoughtfulness in your relationship also requires active listening. Learning what stimulates your partner mentally, what supports them emotionally, and feeds them spiritually, creates a high level of quality energy that is sure to translate into the bedroom. **Finding ways to bring more joy into each other's lives** based on what you're learning about each other is crucial to a healthy relationship.

Creating quality time outside of the bedroom translates to quality time in the bedroom. When you're connected, present, and charged with love, power, and arousing energy it ignites and excites. Mental and spiritual stimulation yields a deeper physical/sexual experience.

In contrast, the ego is self-serving when it comes to sex. It wants what it wants when it wants it, regardless of how the other person feels. So, be good to each other, be mindful, be spontaneous, and free. Never try to meet sex quotas or pressure each other. Continue to keep working and **strive to make love outside of the bedroom as much as you can.** Let that energy stir up from within and then act on the inspiration.

Infidelity

I'd like to touch on the subject of infidelity because it is running rampant through marriages, and tearing them apart.

Infidelity is not caused by the other person. I repeat. Infidelity is not caused by the other person. As was explained earlier, you cannot blame the other person for your own actions. Infidelity is a symptom of something that one is not giving to themselves and usually stems from a betrayal of one's own heart. It is often based on a lack of self-love, a lack of self-respect, and a lack of self-honor.

Insecurities, ego, and fear, produce infidelity. The soul does not. Your soul would rather end the marriage peacefully instead of participating in infidelity, which is why it's so important to gain insight into your emotional baggage, as well as getting to know what's in your heart and your partner's heart.

A betrayal of the heart will show up in some form of betrayal somewhere else. When you discover the desires of your heart, it is then your job to **build the strength, courage, and confidence to bring forth those desires.** Operating in this manner leaves no room for infidelity.

Redefining Marriage

Chapter 6
Building a Vision for Your Marriage

Consider creating a vision for your marriage. Talk to your partner about what you would like to experience through your marriage, what you envision your marriage to be, what it looks and feels like, and how you can support each other in becoming great!

Marriage is a spiritual endeavor and because it is spiritual, it is fluid and can change and take on many different forms (for the better). Marriage is also a service-based relationship, although at the end of the day, it is self-sacrificing. It is important to remember that together, you and your partner are each other's helpmates. The following are some tips for creating a high powered, high energy union.

Put God First

Continue to seek out and get to know God's ways and develop a strong desire to **understand the plan He has for you.**

You will both benefit from having a personal relationship with Him first. He speaks to you in the quiet, which is why quiet time alone in your marriage is so important.

Redefining Marriage

As fantastic as your partner is, putting your mate above God will keep you running around in circles. Strive to have a relationship with yourself and God first and then let that love spill over into your marriage.

Perfect Structure

God < You < Partner
Not: Partner < You < God

God gives direction and guidance, joy and peace, He is all knowing and loving, and putting Him at the head of your marriage keeps your marriage strong, honest, loving, and growing.

Mindfulness

The type of energy you put into the marriage is the type of energy you will get out of the marriage. Is it a spirit of joy, hope, spontaneity, adventure and support? Or is it laced with hidden insecurities, fears, doubts, worries? Being mindful and intentional from the start will yield you a great return.

Marriage is an Extension

You are not your marriage. Marriage is an extension of you. It needs to be fed, nurtured, and treated with loving kindness and respect just as much as you as an individual need to be fed and nurtured. The key to effortlessly nurturing your marriage is to continuously **find ways to nurture yourself in mind, body and spirit.**

Operate in Truth

Speak up in your marriage. Speak what is true for you and what's in your heart and give your mate the space to speak what's true for them. Creating a union based in truth leaves no room for lies. Speak to each other with heart from the heart. This takes practice and at times will be uncomfortable but the more you do it the better you'll get at it. Not speaking your truth will only box you in, making you feel as though you are a trapped prisoner in your own home. So speak up! No one ever benefits when you silence yourself. **Care about how you feel.** Your marriage is meant to be a freeing experience. Always strive to speak from the heart.

The following are some questions for you and your partner to think about as it pertains to creating a vision and a feeling for your marriage. There are a set of questions for you and another set for your partner. Fill them out separately and then come together to create something beautiful and harmonious.

Your marriage is unique to you and may not look like anyone else's, which is the beauty of it all.

Redefining Marriage

Questions for You

What vision do you have for your marriage?

How do you want your marriage to feel?

What do you hope to give and receive from the marriage?

What would you like to experience with your partner in this marriage?

Questions for Your Partner

What vision do you have for your marriage?

How do you want your marriage to feel?

What do you hope to give and receive from the marriage?

What would you like to experience with your partner in this marriage?

Redefining Marriage

Chapter 7
A Final Word...

The principles in this book have been designed to inspire you towards diving deeper into the soul of both you and your partner simultaneously. Building a conscious and harmonious relationship is a journey and therefore, the healthier you are mentally, spiritually and emotionally, the healthier your relationship will become.

My hope is that you build a foundation of unconditional love that is so strong; the ego has no way of seeping in and causing discord. In short, dissolve your fears and insecurities, follow your heart, take good care of each other's souls, and you'll witness magic happening over and over again.

Sending you much love on your Spiritual Journey of Oneness.

Redefining Marriage

About The Author

Tori Player is a Workshop Leader, Teacher and Mentor, who specializes in strengthening the spirit and healing the heart. Her mission is to guide individuals and couples through self-healing methods that sheds light on the manner in which we function, thus helping them live more fully from the inside out. Based on Tori's teachings, when we know who we are at a soul level and when we learn the difference between soul and ego, we are then in a position to create greater lives, greater experiences, greater love, and greater relationships.

Her passion for healing modalities and her love for deepening the connection to Self is an inspiration to all those that work with her.

You can find her on Instagram @tori.player and her website www.toriplayer.com

Redefining Marriage

www.ingramcontent.com/pod-product-compliance
Lightning Source LLC
Chambersburg PA
CBHW020548080526
44583CB00013B/1053